FLORIE SAINT-VAL

Translated by Sarah Ardizzone

LIFITO

THE LITTLE

FACTORY

OF ILLUSTRATION

Tate Publishing

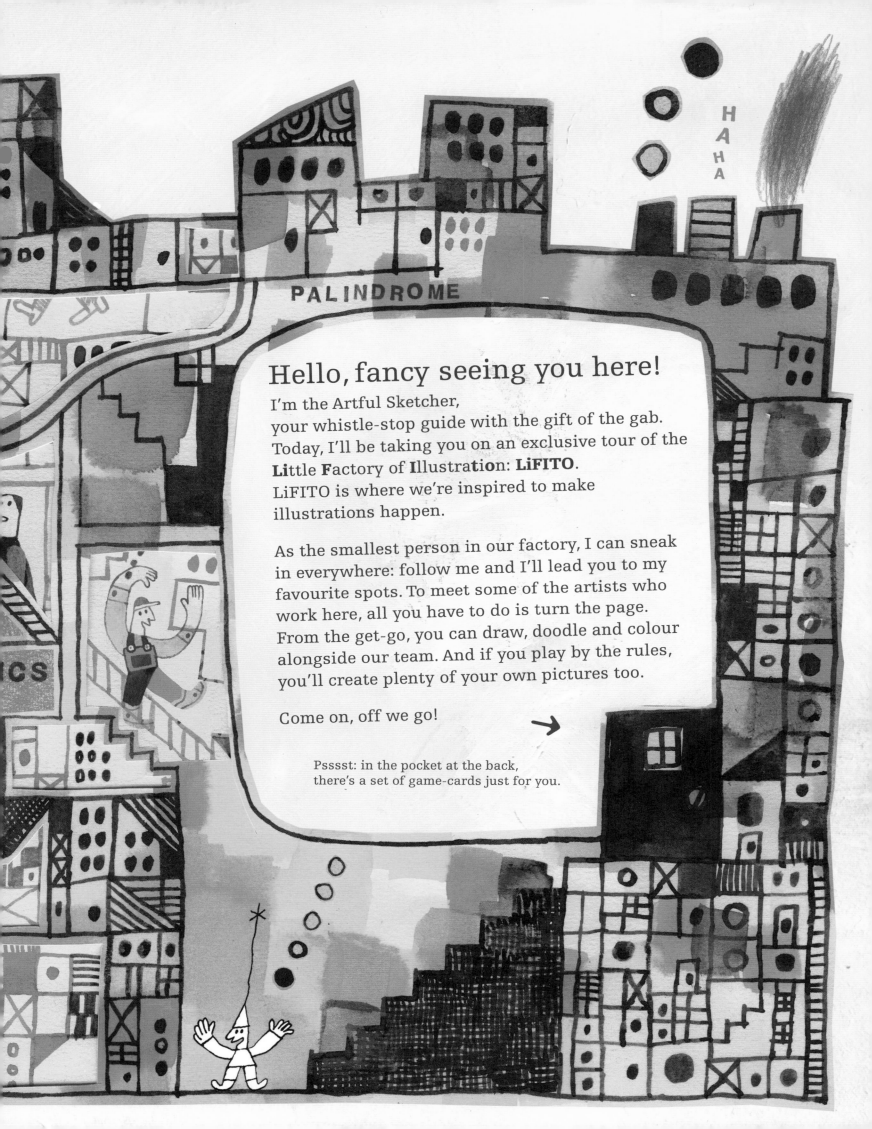

Hello, fancy seeing you here!

I'm the Artful Sketcher,
your whistle-stop guide with the gift of the gab.
Today, I'll be taking you on an exclusive tour of the
Little Factory of Illustration: LiFITO.
LiFITO is where we're inspired to make
illustrations happen.

As the smallest person in our factory, I can sneak
in everywhere: follow me and I'll lead you to my
favourite spots. To meet some of the artists who
work here, all you have to do is turn the page.
From the get-go, you can draw, doodle and colour
alongside our team. And if you play by the rules,
you'll create plenty of your own pictures too.

Come on, off we go! →

Psssst: in the pocket at the back,
there's a set of game-cards just for you.

–Palindrome Portraits–

Let's start by taking the corridor that leads us to the heart of the factory. Along the way, you can admire the gallery of masks handed down to us by our elders: the 'long-in-the-tooth Lifitians'. They're the ones who created LiFITO a long time ago. Back in the day, they used to make peculiar masks as a way of representing themselves. At first glance, they're nothing special, but guess what? These masks are magic.

LAMELIE

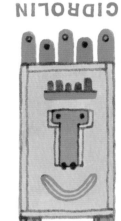

CIDROLIN

RAYMOND QUENELLE

FRANCOIS THE LION

NILE

YIOU

MR GLUG-GLUG

ZAZIE

NOEL LEON

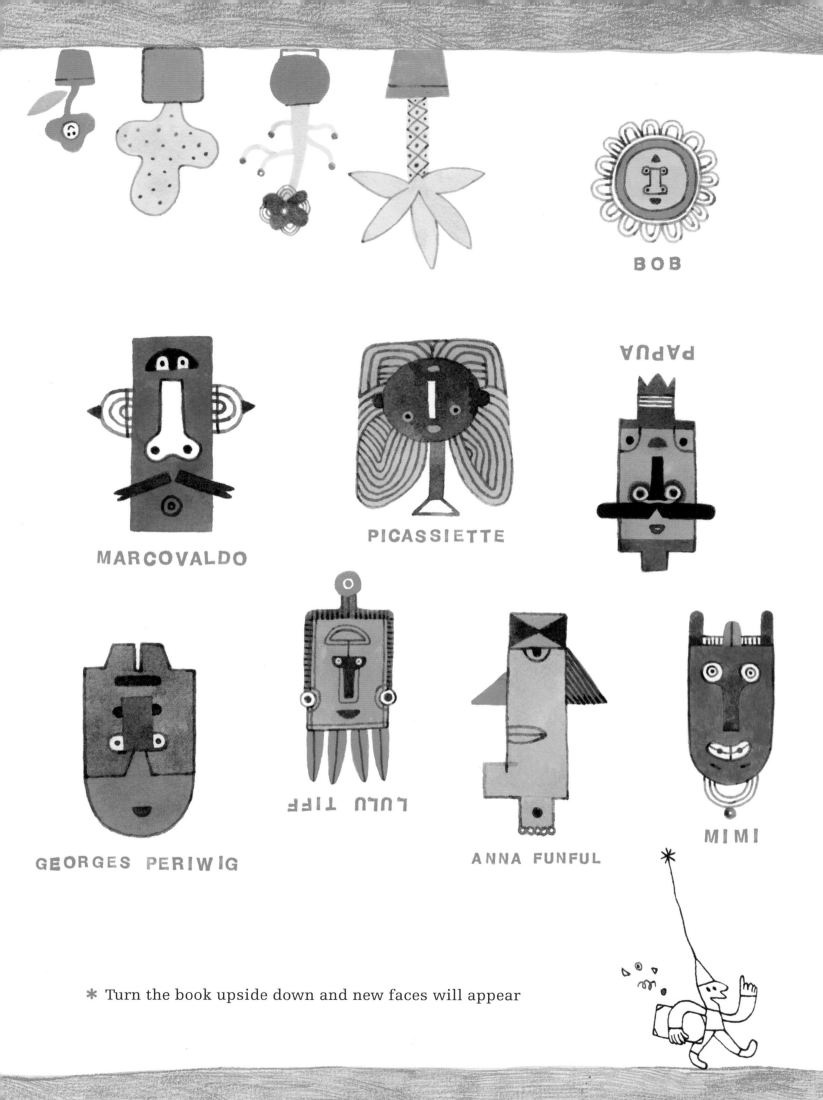

BOB

MARCOVALDO

PICASSIETTE

PAPUA

GEORGES PERIWIG

LULU TIFF

ANNA FUNFUL

MIMI

* Turn the book upside down and new faces will appear

–Reception–

Welcome to the hurly-burly of the factory floor.
Everybody's bustling because there's so much to do today:
delivering the colours, re-stocking the picture machines and handing out the post.
This is a great opportunity to introduce you to my best friends Roxy, Bob and
Jojo, our colouring champions, who've been together since primary school.
There's Doodler too, a colourful artist with prodigious hands.
And Miss Line, whose drawings reveal strokes of genius.

＊ Can you find my friends in the crowd?

my best friends:

Roxy
Bob
Jojo

miss Line

Doodler

– Miss Line –

Miss Line can draw for hours without lifting her pencil or taking her eyes off the page.

She covers sheets of paper with lines and strokes going in every direction. You can tell when she's feeling inspired because she can't help twirling her curly hair.

✳ Can you work out which way leads to the tangled mop on her head?
And which way leads to a pencil-sharpener, a comb or a telephone?
Answers in the box on the opposite page, please!

hello,
Lifito,
can i help you?

mister Comb

mimi
the Pencil
Sharpener

1 _ _ _ _ _ _ _ _ _ _ _ _ _
2 _ _ _ _ _ _ _ _ _ _ _ _ _
3 _ _ _ _ _ _ _ _ _ _ _ _ _
4 _ _ _ _ _ _ _ _ _ _ _ _ _

✳ In a single stroke, and each time without taking your pencil off the page,
can you fill the blank sheets of paper that haven't yet been scrawled on by Miss Line?

-The Colour Fountain-

Roxy, Jojo and Bob are responsible for loading up the colour fountain, where all the factory artists come to refresh their palettes.

Every day, the trio loves to hurtle down the tube-oggans in order to flood this magic supply with new paint.

✳ Can you help my friends fill up the pipes with your favourite colours?

– Doodler and the Patterns –

No prizes for guessing that Doodler is a world expert when it comes to doodling. He uses coloured pencils, paints, crayons, ink and felt-tip pens to turn every scrap of paper he can lay his hands on into a surprising design. He paints splodges, draws dots and creates patterns by shading-in. Plus, he's crafty not only with his fingers but also with his toes.

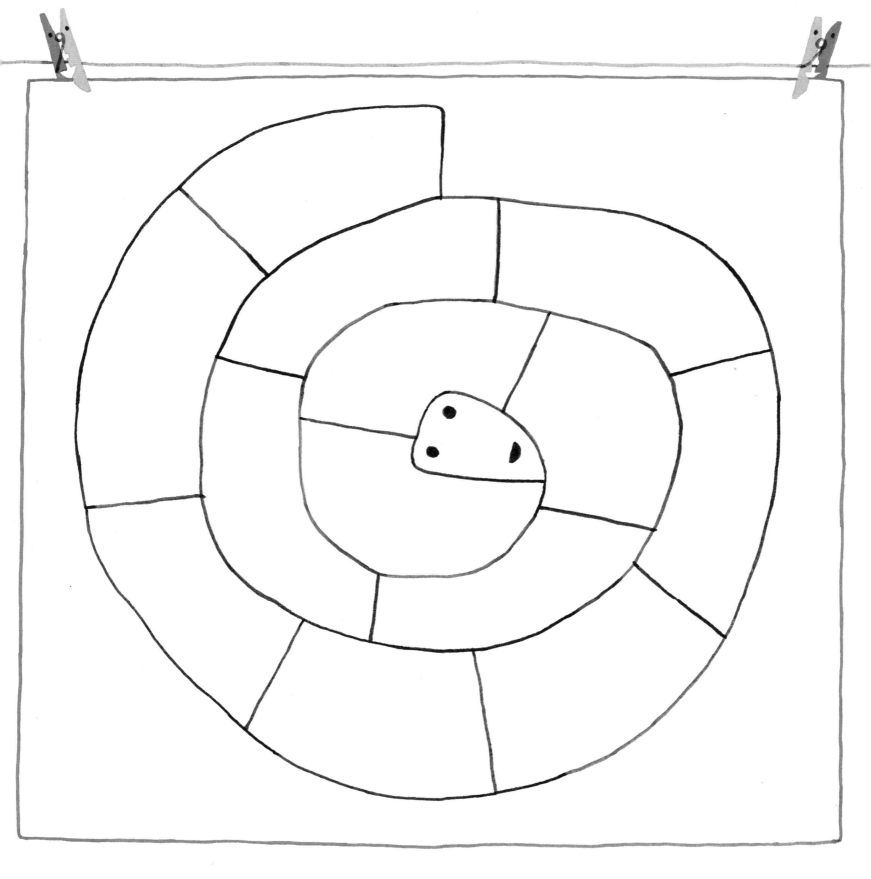

* Why don't you collect all the materials you can find at home, and make your own designs for the sketch that Miss Line gave to Doodler?

Let's flit about the paper room. There's every kind of paper in here: wallpaper, newspaper, gift-wrap, gold leaf, and even sheet music. Today, my larger-than-life friend, Raga Man, has dropped by because he wants to jazz up his old overall.

✳ Cut out stuff you like from old magazines to make Raga's outfit look sharp.

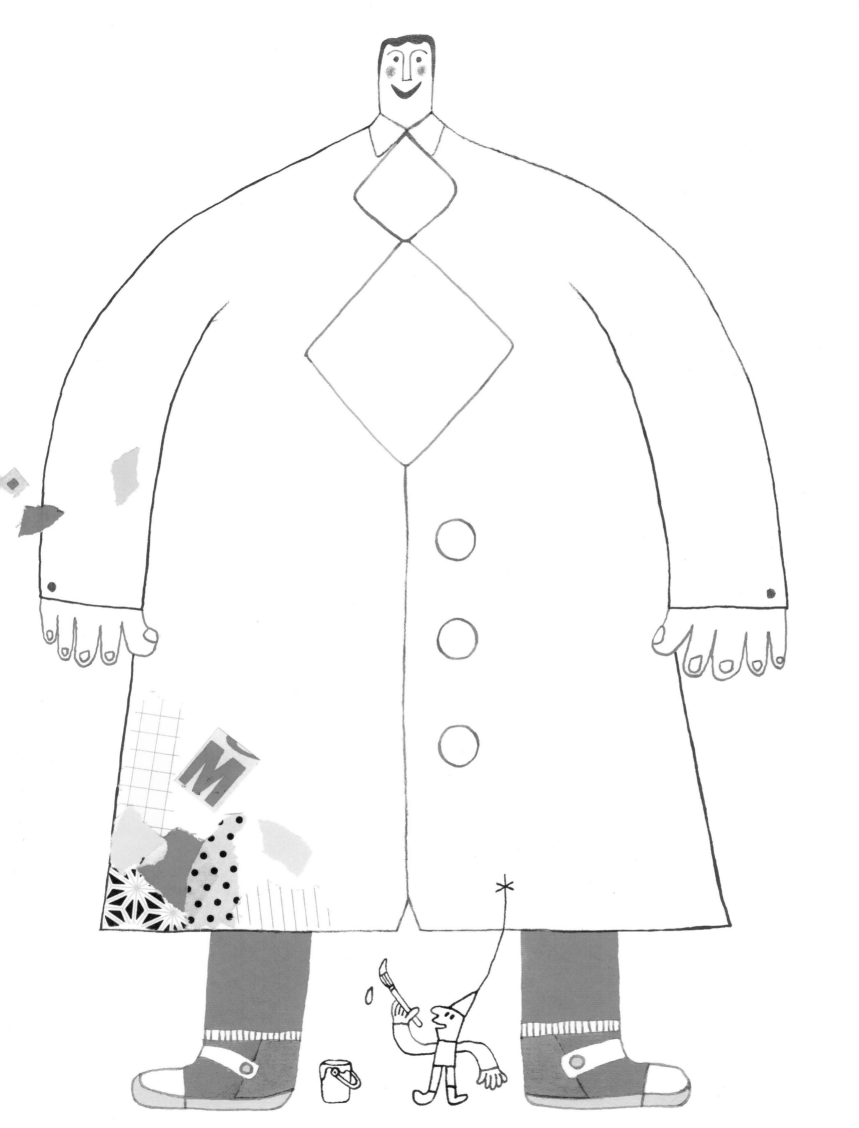

–The Lulugram–

Now I'd like to introduce you to an astonishing game: the Lulugram.
From the seven shapes designed by Lulu, you can create a never-ending supply
of funny characters and bizarre animals.
To get an idea of how many combinations are possible, just pop the pieces
from the game into the Machine of Possibilities.

＊ Rummage in the pocket at the back, where you'll find a puzzle-card to help you design your
own oddball characters.

– Domipics –

It's time for me to introduce you to a famous LiFITO game: 'domipics'.
I bet you've played dominoes before? Well, domipics is kind of like dominoes,
but instead of small dots there are creepy-crawlies.
To play, match the pieces according to the number of creepy-crawly legs.

✳ Back in the pocket, you'll find two game-cards
to help you start your own set of domipics.

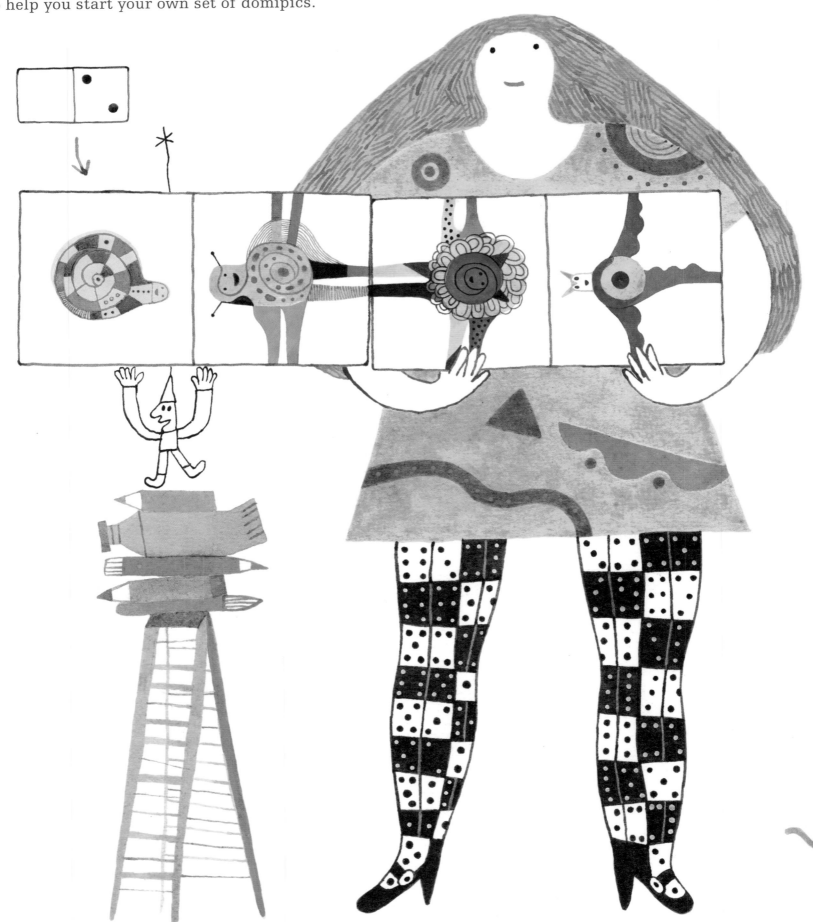

—Alphabet Sculptures—

Here's how it works: each letter of the alphabet corresponds to a coloured geometric shape.
The LiFITO artists assemble these shapes into personalised sculptures for their friends.
Take a look at what Jade has sculpted for her friend Pablo.

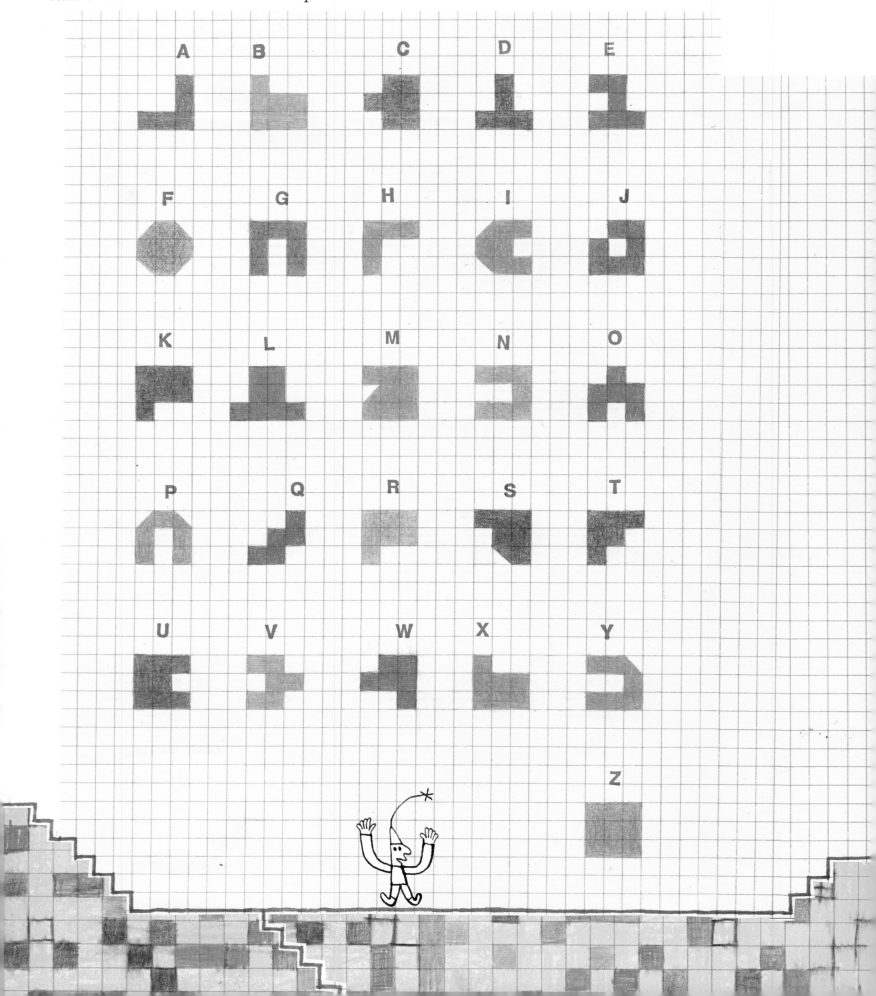

* Build the sculpture of your own name, using your favourite pencils (the squared paper should help).
You can also make sculptures for my friends: Roxy, Raga and Lulu.

* Guess the names hidden behind
these sculptures.

P
A
B
L
O

–A Thousand Billion Faces–

Of all the recent inventions at our factory, one of my favourites is the Machine of A Thousand Billion Faces. The different facial features get scrambled up inside the pipes, the machine randomly ejects them and then: hey presto! The super-sophisticated crayonix can draw a face in seconds flat.

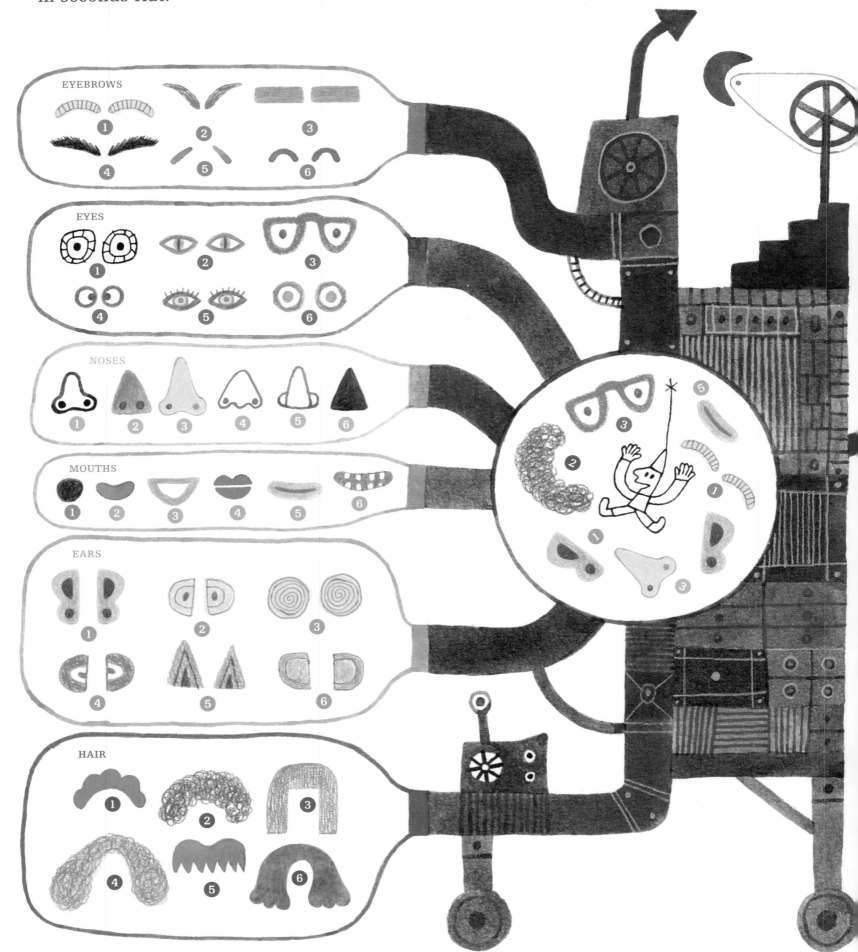

It's easy to create billions of different portraits:
borrow a die from a board game and roll a number between 1 and 6.
If you roll a 3, for example, you must draw the No. 3 eyebrows for your character.
Do the same for the other facial features: eyes, nose, mouth, and so on.

– Symmetrius –

Now I'm taking you to the top of the factory, and out onto the roof.
This is where the wild palindromes come to roost.
Wild palindromes, also known as *Symmetrius*, are very rare birds indeed.
Have you spotted how their bodies are identical on the left and right?

* Finish drawing some of these extraordinary birds, then colour them in.

–Your Office–

And now it's over to you: welcome to your personal office.

* Complete this *Symmetrius* palindrome.

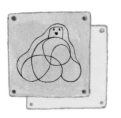

* To discover what's hidden behind Miss Line's latest composition, colour in each section. The dots left by Roxy, Bob and Jojo are your colour code.

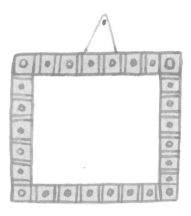

✳ Leave your thumb-
or finger-print here.

✳ Draw your favourite Lifitian.

✳ Make a collage for Lulu's new dress.

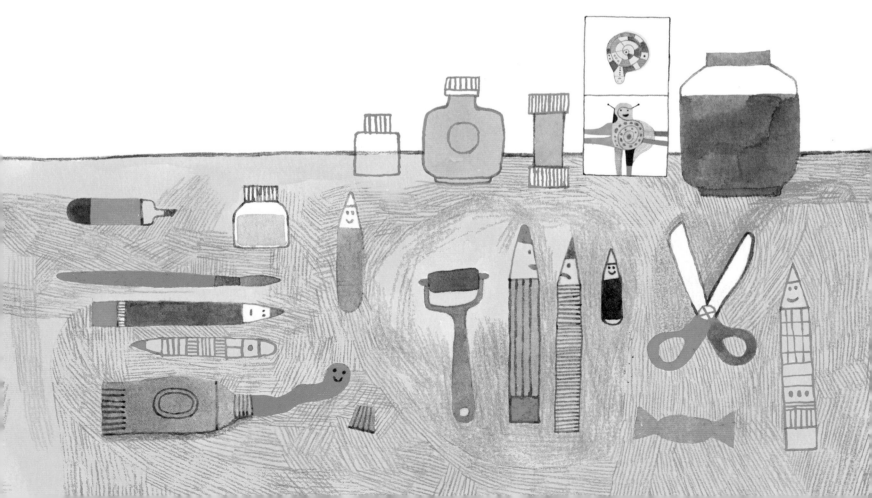

This time, the Lifitians have made masses of outrageous outfits.

* Cut along the dotted lines and swap the pages over to see how many different fancy dress costumes you can produce. What's your favourite combo?

Ta-da! Here comes your surprise.
A major exhibition is being
held in your honour.

* Choose carefully what goes in the frames.
(Who knows when your next show will be?)

HURLY
BURLY

– See You Soon –

It's time to say goodbye.
Oh, all right then, here's one last space for you to draw in:
we'd like your self-portrait, because you're
part of the family now, you're a Lifitian too!

If you fancy another tour of LiFITO, why not see how many of these you can spot along the way?

HU
RLY
BURLY

* Have you noticed how I've lost all my fabulous colours? Well, I'd love someone to colour me in.

Where does LiFITO come from?

The **Li**ttle **F**actory of **I**llustra**t**i**o**n is a cousin of OULIPO, the Workshop of Potential Literature (l'**OU**vroir de **LI**ttérature **PO**tentielle), which was established by two friends in 1960:

François le Lionnais, a great mathematician, and Raymond Queneau, a great writer. The Oulipians and their circle (including Italo Calvino, Georges Perec and Marcel Duchamp, as well as other mathematicians and people of letters) invented some constraints – or rules – to make writing fun.

For example, the Oulipian Georges Perec decided to write a whole book without ever using the letter *e*.

Inspired by Oulipians "tinkering with letters", the Lifitians tinker with pictures by following their own made-up rules.